DISCOVER
Equivalent Fractions

by Brett Kelly

Table of Contents

Introduction

A fraction shows part of a **whole**. A fraction shows part of a **set**. **Equivalent fractions** show the same amount.

I need to know these math words.

denominators

$$\frac{1}{4} = \frac{2}{8}$$

denominator → 4   8 ← denominator

equivalent fractions

$$\frac{2}{4} = \frac{1}{2}$$

Two-fourths is equal to one-half.

numerators

numerator ▸ $\dfrac{1}{4} = \dfrac{2}{8}$ ◂ numerator

set

$\frac{1}{4}$ $\frac{1}{4}$

$\frac{1}{4}$ $\frac{1}{4}$

whole

$\frac{1}{4}$ $\frac{1}{4}$

$\frac{1}{4}$ $\frac{1}{4}$

See the Glossary on page 22.

What Do Equivalent Fractions Show?

Equivalent fractions show the same amount.

equivalent fractions

$$\frac{2}{4} = \frac{1}{2}$$

Two-fourths is equal to one-half.

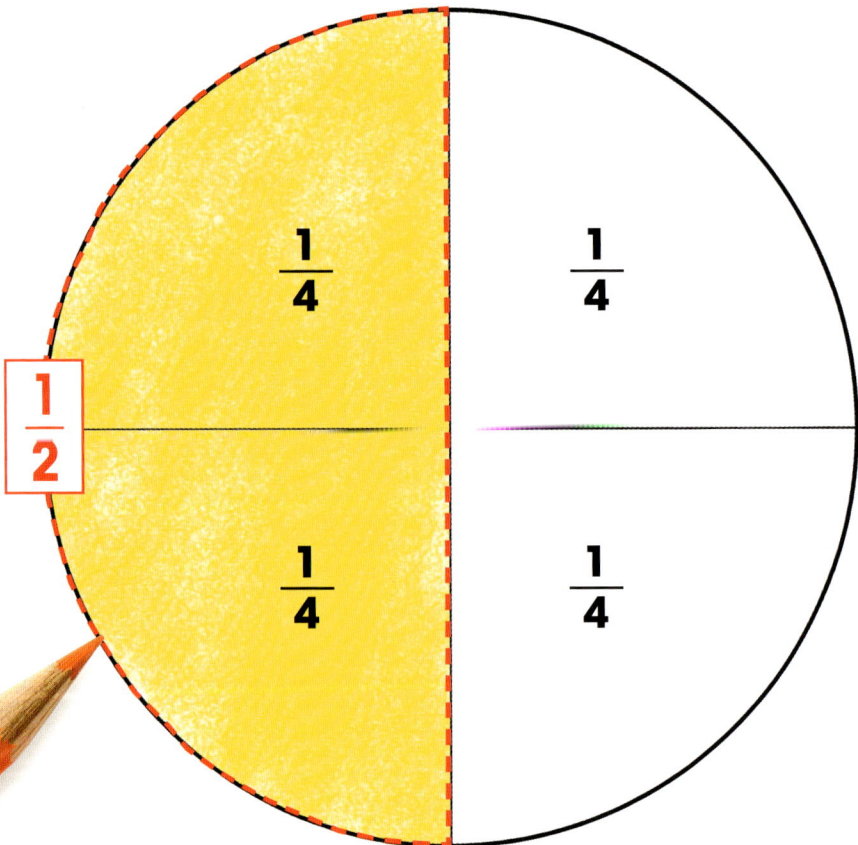

$\frac{1}{4}$	$\frac{1}{4}$
$\frac{1}{4}$	$\frac{1}{4}$

$\frac{1}{2}$

▲ We see the same amount.

Equivalent fractions show parts.

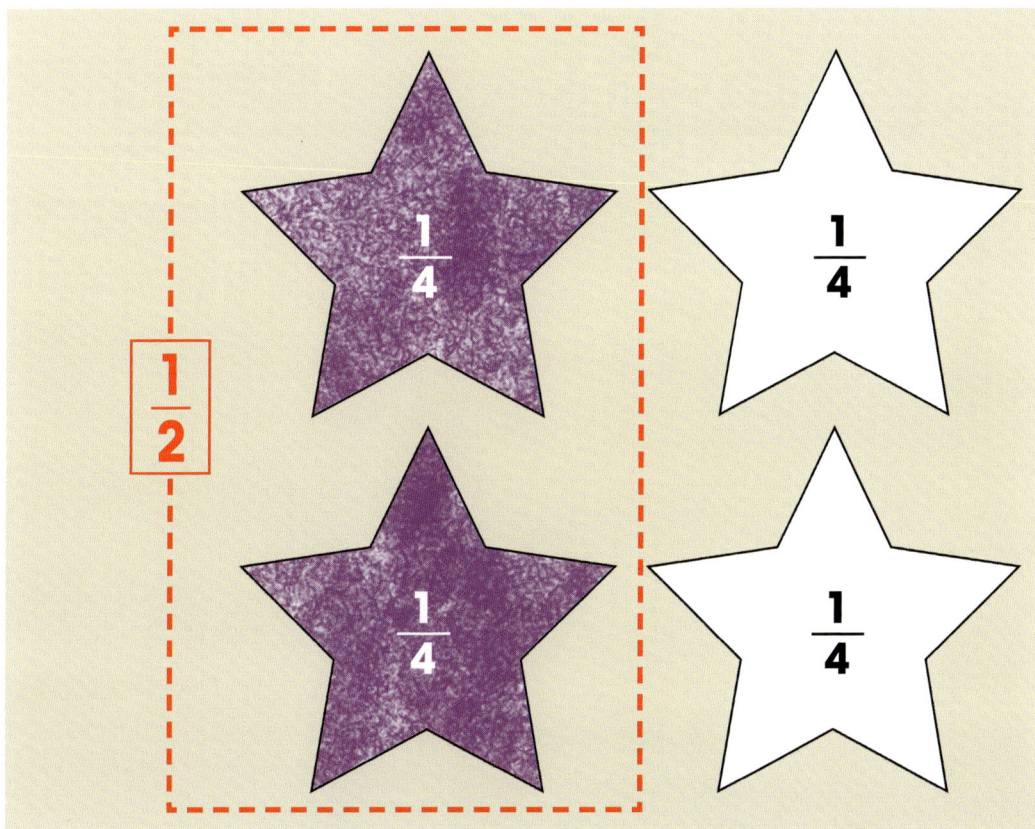

$\frac{1}{2}$ | $\frac{1}{4}$ $\frac{1}{4}$ | $\frac{1}{4}$ $\frac{1}{4}$

▲ We see the same amount.

Did You Know?

A fraction can show part of a whole.
A fraction can show part of a set.

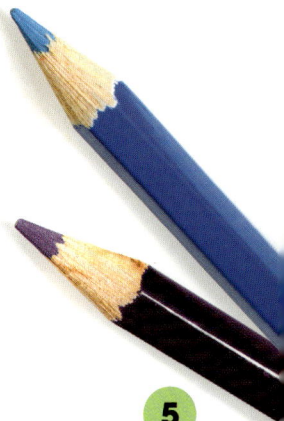

Equivalent fractions show **numerators**.

equivalent fractions

numerator ▶ $\dfrac{2}{8}$ = $\dfrac{1}{4}$ ◀ numerator

Two-eighths is equal to one-fourth.

| $\dfrac{1}{8}$ | $\dfrac{1}{8}$ | $\dfrac{1}{8}$ | $\dfrac{1}{8}$ |
| $\dfrac{1}{8}$ | $\dfrac{1}{8}$ | $\dfrac{1}{8}$ | $\dfrac{1}{8}$ |

$\dfrac{1}{4}$

▲ We see numerators.

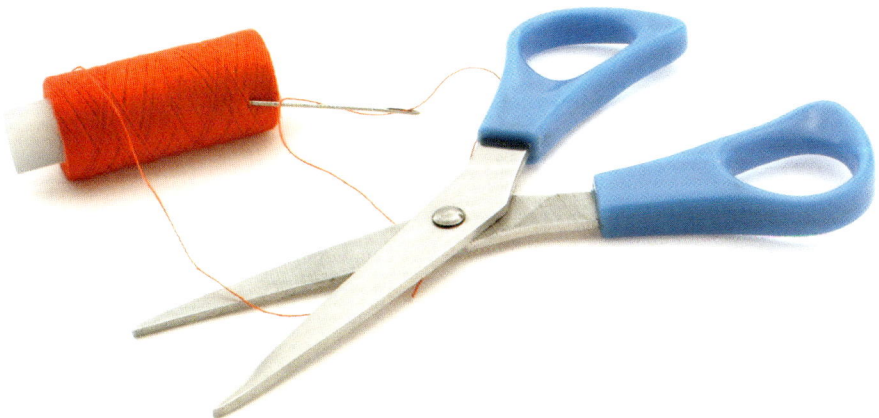

Equivalent fractions show **denominators**.

equivalent fractions

denominator ➤ $\dfrac{1}{5}$ $=$ $\dfrac{2}{10}$ ◀ denominator

One-fifth   is equal to   two-tenths.

1				
$\dfrac{1}{5}$	$\dfrac{1}{5}$	$\dfrac{1}{5}$	$\dfrac{1}{5}$	$\dfrac{1}{5}$

$\dfrac{1}{10}$	$\dfrac{1}{10}$	$\dfrac{1}{10}$	$\dfrac{1}{10}$	$\dfrac{1}{10}$	$\dfrac{1}{10}$	$\dfrac{1}{10}$	$\dfrac{1}{10}$	$\dfrac{1}{10}$	$\dfrac{1}{10}$

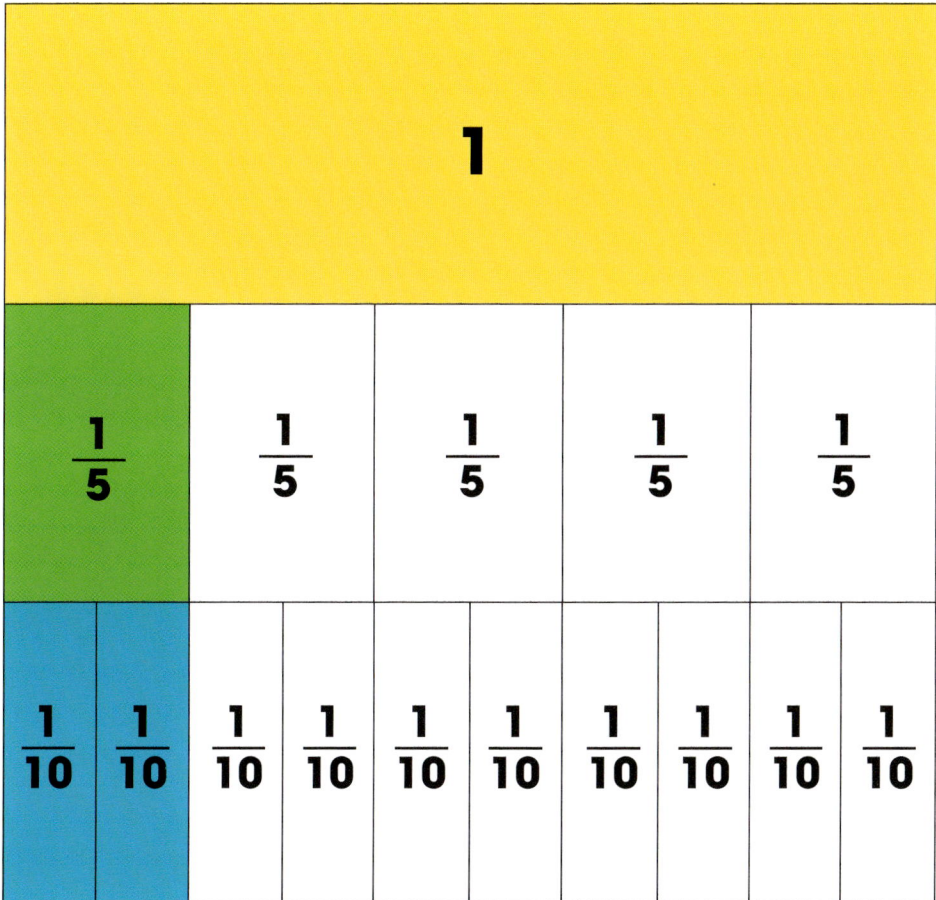

▲ We see denominators.

Equivalent fractions show part of a set.

equivalent fractions

$$\frac{2}{6} = \frac{1}{3}$$

Two-sixths   is equal to   one-third.

▲ We see the same amount.

Equivalent fractions show part of a whole.

equivalent fractions

$$\frac{6}{8} = \frac{3}{4}$$

Six-eighths is equal to three-fourths.

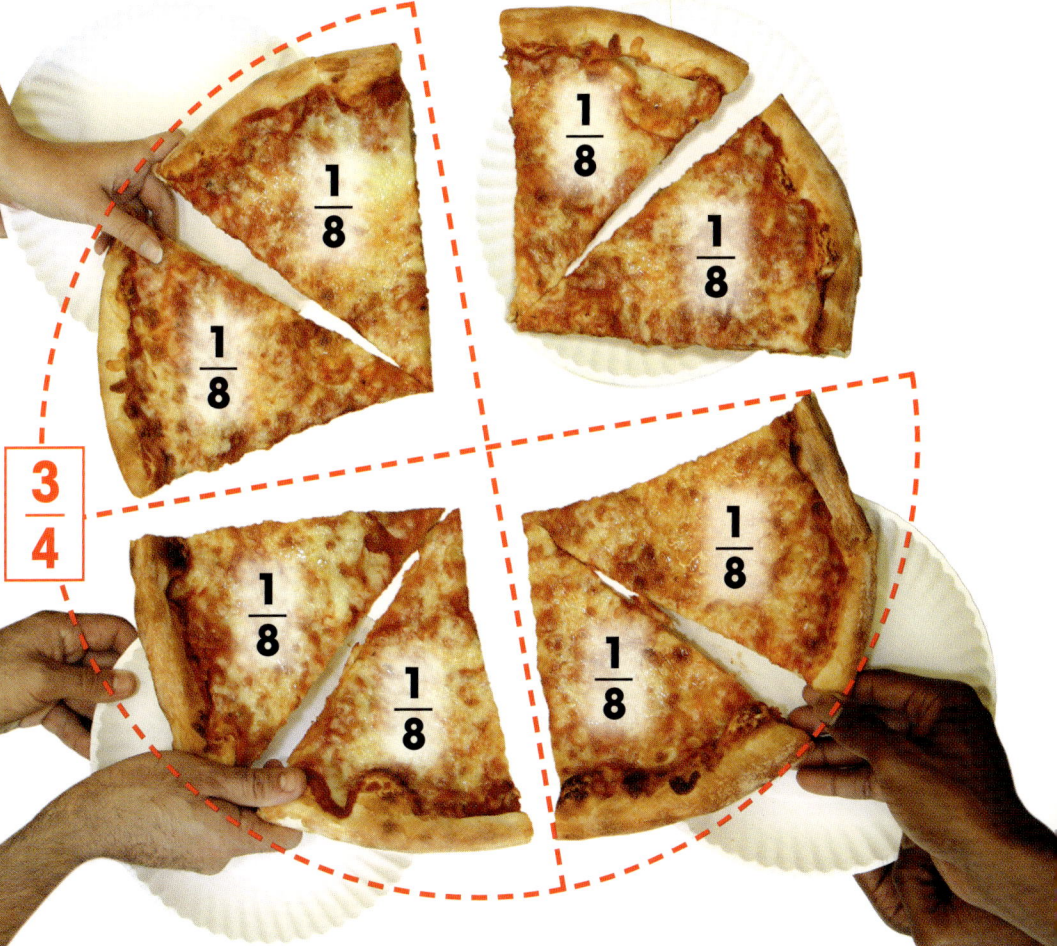

$\frac{1}{8}$ $\frac{1}{8}$ $\frac{1}{8}$ $\frac{1}{8}$ $\frac{1}{8}$ $\frac{1}{8}$ $\frac{1}{8}$ $\frac{1}{8}$

$\frac{3}{4}$

▲ We see the same amount.

9

What Fractions Are Equal to One-Half?

Two-fourths is equal to one-half. $\frac{2}{4} = \frac{1}{2}$.

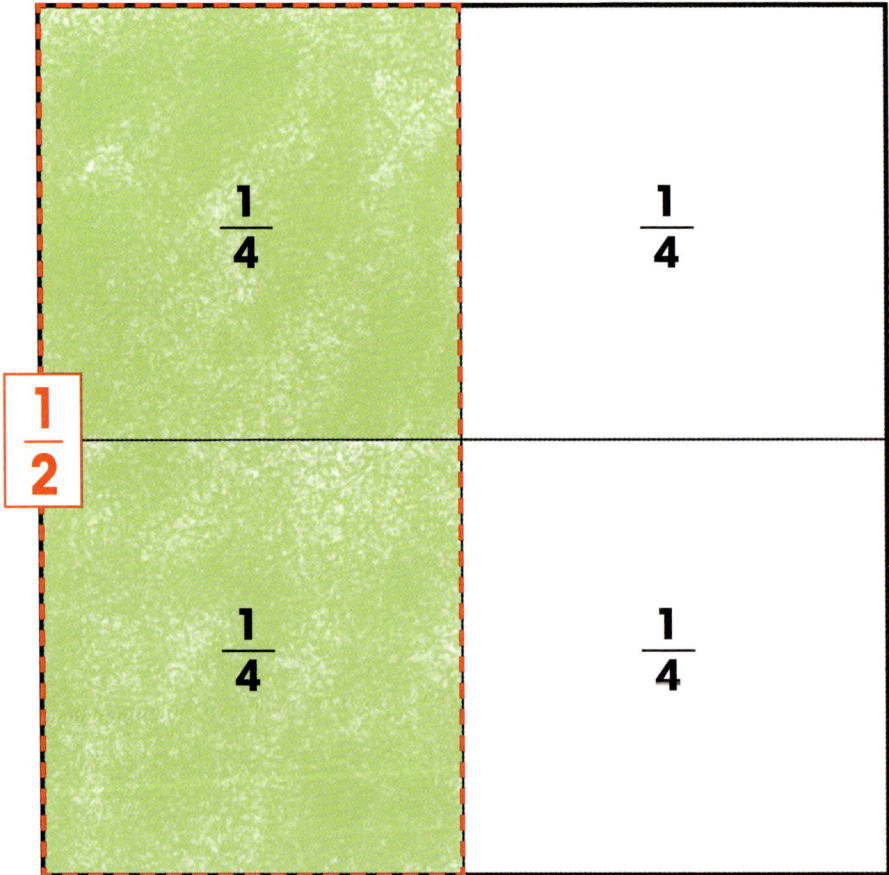

$\frac{1}{2}$

$\frac{1}{4}$ $\frac{1}{4}$

$\frac{1}{4}$ $\frac{1}{4}$

▲ Two-fourths and one-half are equivalent fractions.

Three-sixths is equal to one-half. $\frac{3}{6} = \frac{1}{2}$.

$\frac{1}{2}$

$\frac{1}{6}$ $\frac{1}{6}$

$\frac{1}{6}$ $\frac{1}{6}$

$\frac{1}{6}$ $\frac{1}{6}$

▲ **Three-sixths and one-half are equivalent fractions.**

Did You Know?

You can find equivalent fractions on a ruler.

$\frac{1}{2}$

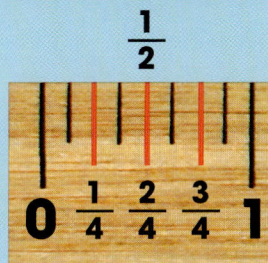

0 $\frac{1}{4}$ $\frac{2}{4}$ $\frac{3}{4}$ 1

Four-eighths is equal to one-half. $\frac{4}{8} = \frac{1}{2}$.

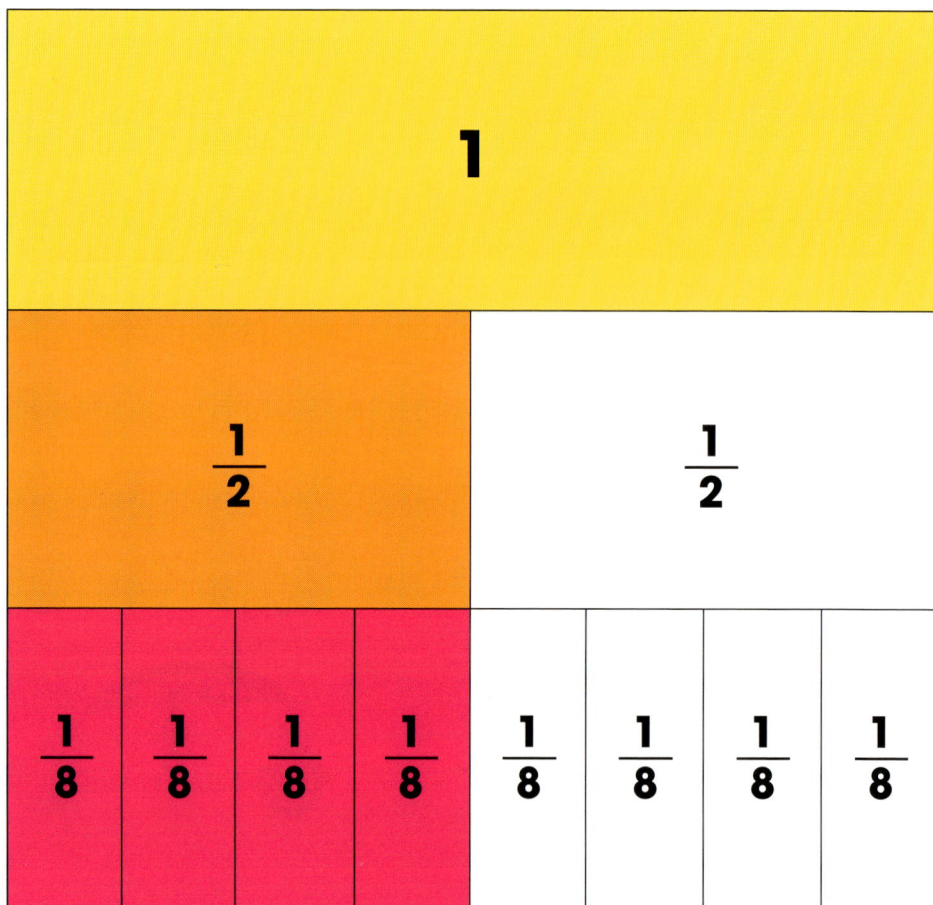

1	
$\frac{1}{2}$	$\frac{1}{2}$
$\frac{1}{8}$ $\frac{1}{8}$ $\frac{1}{8}$ $\frac{1}{8}$	$\frac{1}{8}$ $\frac{1}{8}$ $\frac{1}{8}$ $\frac{1}{8}$

▲ **Four-eighths and one-half are equivalent fractions.**

equivalent fractions

$$\frac{4}{8} = \frac{1}{2}$$

Four-eighths is equal to one-half.

Five-tenths is equal to one-half. $\frac{5}{10} = \frac{1}{2}$.

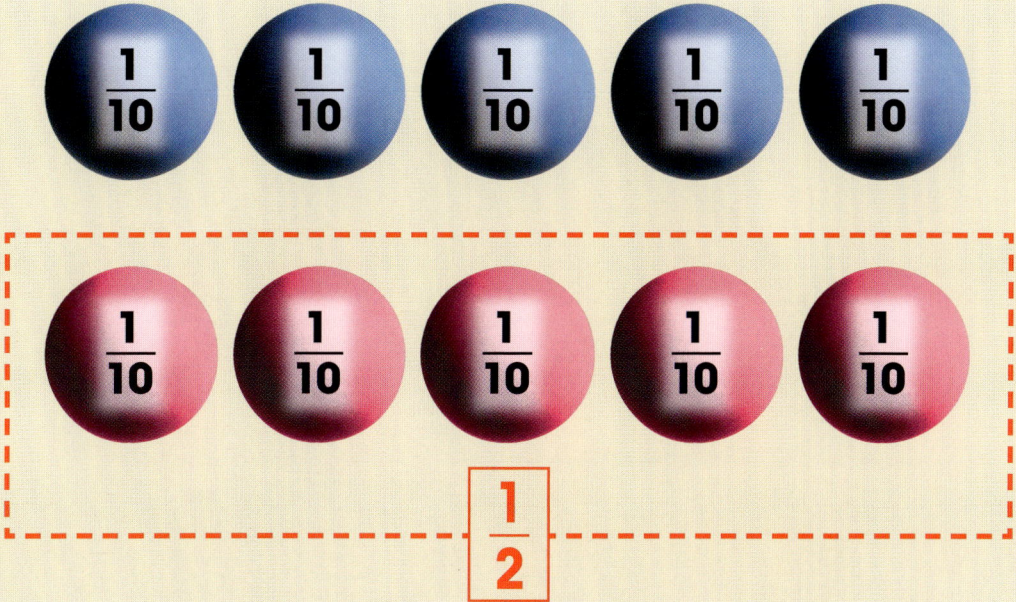

▲ Five-tenths and one-half are equivalent fractions.

equivalent fractions

$$\frac{5}{10} = \frac{1}{2}$$

Five-tenths is equal to one-half.

What Are Some Other Equivalent Fractions?

Two-sixths is equal to one-third. $\frac{2}{6} = \frac{1}{3}$.

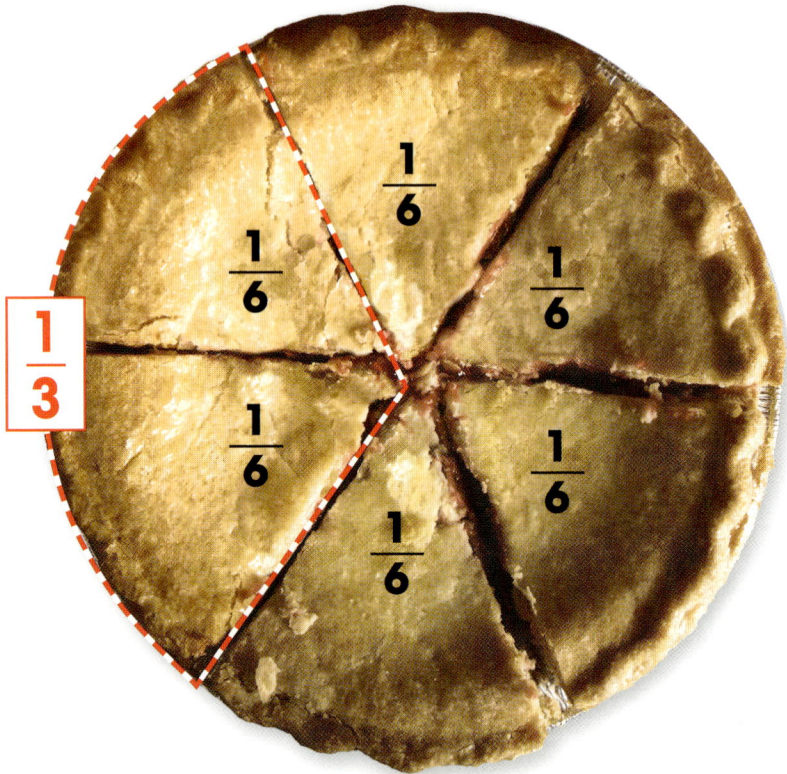

▲ Two-sixths and one-third are equivalent fractions.

equivalent fractions

$$\frac{2}{6} = \frac{1}{3}$$

Two-sixths   is equal to   one-third.

Two-thirds is equal to four-sixths. $\frac{2}{3} = \frac{4}{6}$.

$\frac{2}{3}$

$\frac{1}{6}$ $\frac{1}{6}$ $\frac{1}{6}$ $\frac{1}{6}$ $\frac{1}{6}$ $\frac{1}{6}$

▲ Two-thirds and four-sixths are equivalent fractions.

equivalent fractions

$$\frac{2}{3} = \frac{4}{6}$$

Two-thirds is equal to four-sixths.

Three-thirds is equal to six-sixths. $\frac{3}{3} = \frac{6}{6}$.

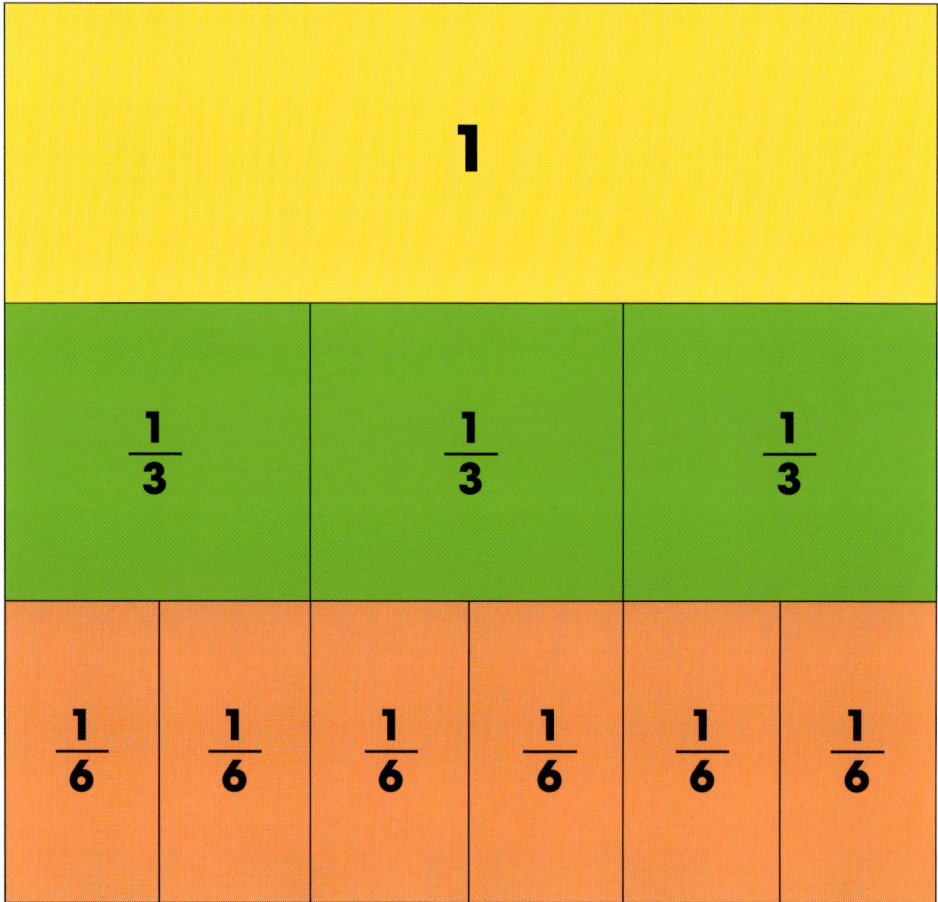

1		
$\frac{1}{3}$	$\frac{1}{3}$	$\frac{1}{3}$
$\frac{1}{6}$ $\frac{1}{6}$	$\frac{1}{6}$ $\frac{1}{6}$	$\frac{1}{6}$ $\frac{1}{6}$

▲ **Three-thirds and six-sixths
are equivalent fractions.**

equivalent fractions

$$\frac{3}{3} = \frac{6}{6}$$

Three-thirds is equal to six-sixths.

Two-eighths is equal to one-fourth. $\frac{2}{8} = \frac{1}{4}$.

▲ **Two-eighths and one-fourth are equivalent fractions.**

equivalent fractions

$$\frac{2}{8} = \frac{1}{4}$$

Two-eighths is equal to one-fourth.

Solve This

How many boxes are red? Write a fraction to show your answer. Write an equivalent fraction.

Conclusion

Equivalent fractions show the same amount.

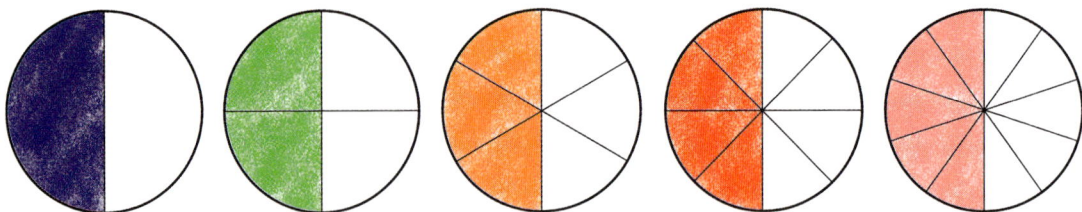

$$\frac{1}{2} = \frac{2}{4} = \frac{3}{6} = \frac{4}{8} = \frac{5}{10}$$

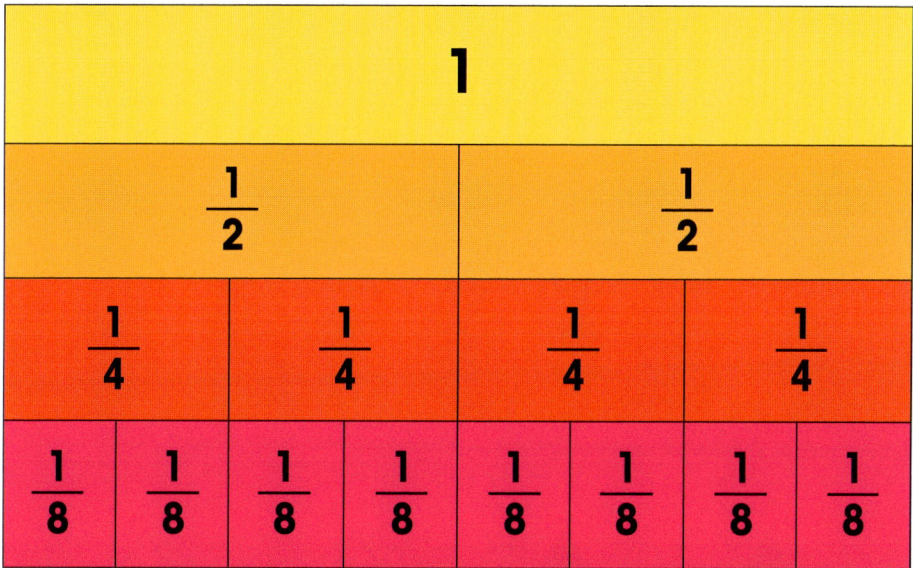

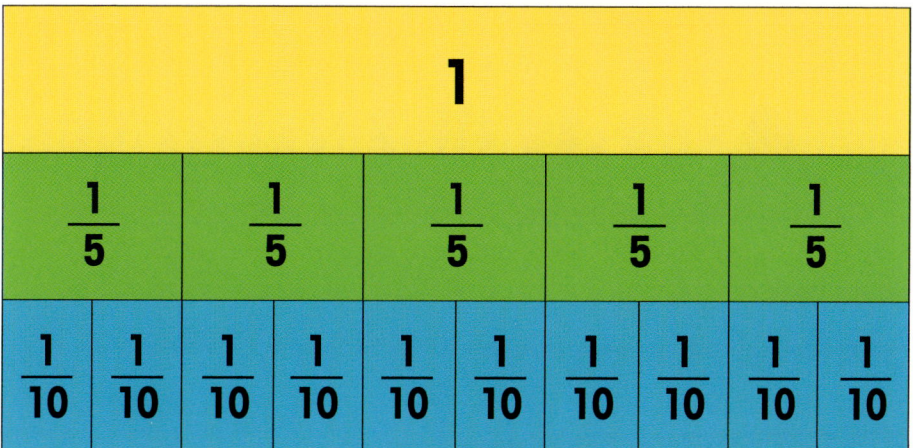

Math Talk

Talk about equivalent fractions.

1.

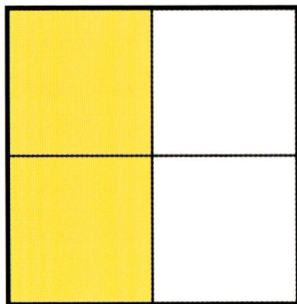

? is equal to ? .
? and ? are equivalent fractions.

2.

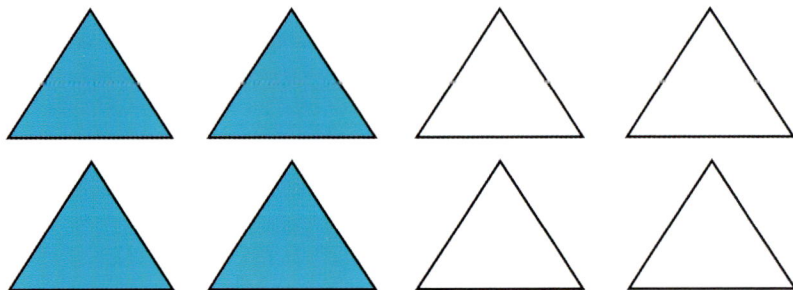

? is equal to ? .
? and ? are equivalent fractions.

3.

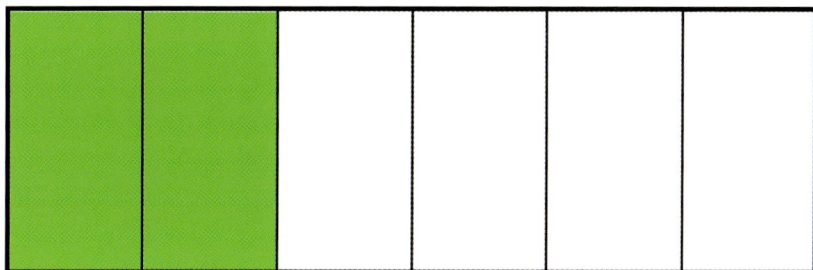

? is equal to ? .

? and ? are equivalent fractions.

4.

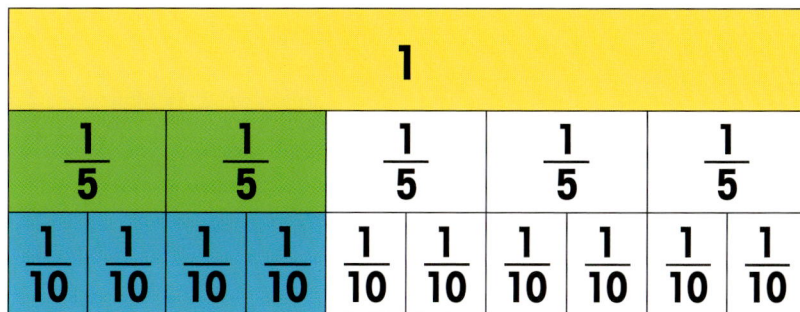

	1				
$\frac{1}{5}$	$\frac{1}{5}$	$\frac{1}{5}$	$\frac{1}{5}$	$\frac{1}{5}$	
$\frac{1}{10}$ $\frac{1}{10}$ $\frac{1}{10}$ $\frac{1}{10}$	$\frac{1}{10}$ $\frac{1}{10}$	$\frac{1}{10}$ $\frac{1}{10}$	$\frac{1}{10}$ $\frac{1}{10}$		

? is equal to ? .

? and ? are equivalent fractions.

Glossary

$$\underset{\text{denominator}}{\quad} \frac{1}{4} = \frac{2}{8} \underset{\text{denominator}}{\quad}$$

denominators the numbers below the bars

*Equivalent fractions show **denominators**.*

$$\frac{2}{4} = \frac{1}{2}$$

equivalent fractions fractions that name the same amount

***Equivalent fractions** show the same amount.*

$$\underset{\text{numerator}}{\quad} \frac{1}{4} = \frac{2}{8} \underset{\text{numerator}}{\quad}$$

numerators the numbers above the bars

*Equivalent fractions show **numerators**.*

set a group of objects or numbers

*A fraction shows part of a **set**.*

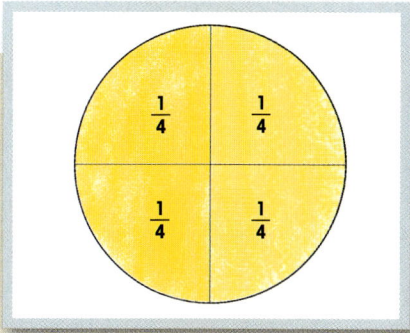

whole the entire region

A fraction shows part of a whole.

Index

After you read . . .

DISCOVER
Equivalent Fractions

Tell what you know about equivalent fractions.

1. Tell what equivalent fractions show.

2. Tell what fractions are equal to one-half.

3. Tell some other equivalent fractions.